CLB 1364
Published in Great Britain 1985 by Crown Books.
Crown Books is a registered imprint of Colour Library Books Ltd.
© 1985 Illustrations and text: Colour Library Books Ltd.,
    Guildford, Surrey, England.
Filmsetting by Acesetters Ltd., Richmond, Surrey, England.
Produced by AGSA, in Barcelona, Spain.
Printed and bound in Barcelona, Spain by Rieusset and Eurobinder.
ISBN 0 86283 323 X

BRITAIN
FROM THE AIR

CROWN BOOKS

Previous pages: the magnificent complex
of buildings at Westminster, on the banks
of the River Thames. The oldest building
is Westminster Hall, which was built for
King William Rufus nine centuries ago. It
now forms part of the Palace of
Westminster, built after 1834 as the
permanent home of Parliament and
government offices. The great Gothic-
style building was designed by Sir Charles
Barry and Augustus Pugin and contains
over a thousand rooms and two miles of
corridors. Westminster Abbey (right
foreground) is the setting for the
coronation of British sovereigns. It has
performed this function since the
Christmas Day coronation of William the
Conqueror in 1066, though the building
has been rebuilt and altered many times in
the intervening years.

These pages: the beautiful Cathedral of
Canterbury, Kent. Though largely of
mediaeval date, principally the 11th and
14th centuries, the Cathedral is the direct
descendant of the monastery founded
here in AD 597 by St Augustine by
permission of Aethelberht, King of Kent.

Overleaf: the Thames-side town of
Marlow, visited by Jerome K. Jerome's
Three Men in a Boat in the last century, is a
pleasant blend of old and new. The
charming High Street runs down to the
river past the lines of shops and houses
before crossing the suspension bridge of
1829. The church of St Peter, by the
bridge, contains a mummified hand
alleged to be that of St James the Apostle.

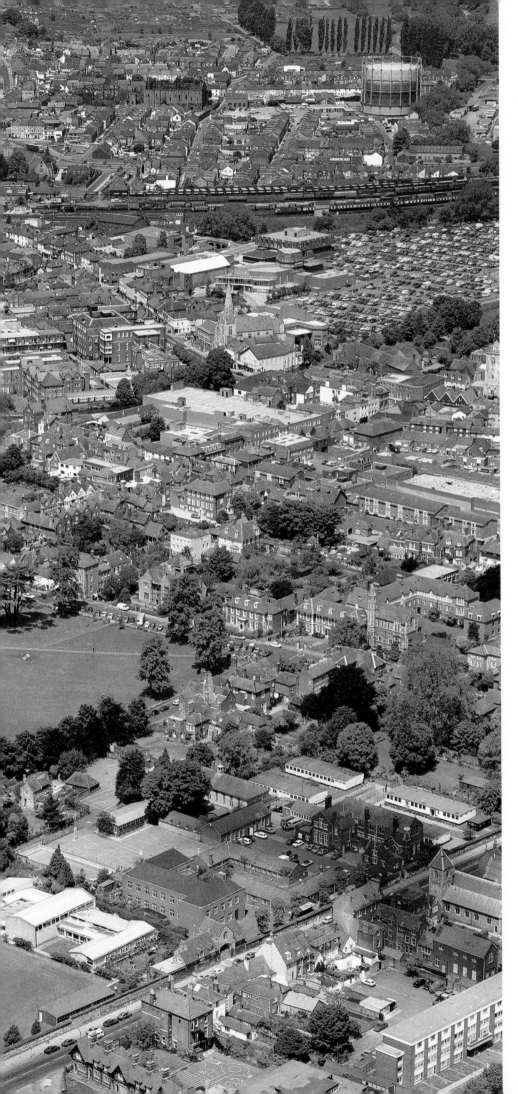

First entering history as a fortified border town in the long wars with the Vikings more than a millennium ago, Oxford (previous pages) did not become a seat of learning until the 12th century. The centre of the city is today mainly given over to the beautiful stone buildings of the various colleges, with their mullioned windows and lofty spires. The town is no longer as dependent upon the colleges for its prosperity as it was at the beginning of the last century, for during this century numerous factories and workshops have appeared in and around Oxford.

When the ancient, hill-top city of Old Sarum was abandoned in the thirteenth century the new Cathedral of Salisbury (these pages) was built on the watermeads of the Avon. The cathedral is unique among those of mediaeval England in having been built in just one period (1220-1266), the only exception being the 404-foot-tall spire which was added a century later and which for many years was the tallest structure in the world.

Overleaf: Towan Head, fringed by foam-spattered waves, is one of the most rugged and beautiful promontories in the vicinity of Newquay on Cornwall's north coast.

Though it dates back to the Roman city of Aquae Sulis and has a mediaeval abbey at its heart, Bath (previous pages) is known as the city of Beau Nash, the Georgian dandy. It was as a centre of high society that Bath came to prominence, and during this period that it acquired its finest architecture. Today, the fine Georgian streets and houses remain, but the city is now more concerned with light industry, tourism and cricket than with fashionable intrigue.

These pages: St Mary's, the largest of the Isles of Scilly. The islands belong to the Duchy of Cornwall, presently held by Prince Charles, and have traditionally relied upon flowers for most of their prosperity. The islands are linked to the Cornish mainland, some 25 miles distant, by both sea and air, a fact which has helped their development as tourist resorts.

Overleaf: the mellow Cotswold village of Bourton-on-the-Water, whose layout is dictated by the tiny River Windrush which runs beside the main street. At intervals the stream is crossed by miniature stone bridges connecting the delightful Cotswold stone houses.

Previous pages: Birmingham is one of the oldest and greatest of Britain's industrial cities. As far back as the Civil War the town was a major producer of arms and by 1762 a single factory was employing a thousand workers but it was not until 1832 that Birmingham recieved its first Member of Parliament. The oldest inhabited part of the city is the Bull Ring, from which the town spread out in Tudor times. Today, the Bull Ring (left foreground) is one of the most impressive shopping centres in the country.

These pages: Ross-on-Wye stands above the River Wye in the Archenfield region of Hereford and Worcester. The picturesque cluster of houses and shops, centred around the tiny market triangle, is clearly separate from the green fields which surround it and the graceful, modern bridge which carries the main road across the Wye.

Overleaf: Stratford-upon-Avon, Warwickshire, is famous as the birthplace of William Shakespeare. The house in which he is reputed to have been born still stands in Henley Street, as does the church (right of picture) in which he is buried, while on the banks of the Avon, near the 15th century bridge, the Royal Shakespeare Theatre has been built in his memory.

On the night of 14th November, 1940 bombs fell from the sky and Coventry (previous pages) was engulfed in destruction. Of all the buildings which were destroyed that night the loss of none was felt more keenly than that of the great mediaeval cathedral, which was reduced to a roofless shell (centre of picture). In 1962 the new cathedral of pink sandstone was completed, adjacent to the ruins of the old, to become one of the most famous modern churches. The rest of the city also recovered from the war to regain its place of great industrial importance.

These pages: the tiny cathedral city of St David's was called Menevia when St David became Bishop and died here during the 6th century. The fine cathedral, which stands in a hollow beneath the city, dates mainly from the 12th century, though restoration work has often been necessary. Also built during the mediaeval period was the Bishop's Palace and the College of St Mary, which now stand in ruins before the cathedral's west front.

Overleaf: the romantic Rheidol Valley, where the sinuous river winds its way through the wooded valley, in Dyfed.

The heart of Welsh Rugby lies at Cardiff Arms Park (previous pages), where the great internationals are played and the singing reaches its musical climax. The rate of growth of the city has been phenomenal over the past hundred years, progressing from little more than a large village to the capital of the Principality of Wales.

An area which boomed earlier than Cardiff was the coal-rich region of South Wales, in particular the Rhondda (these pages). In 1801 the population of the valleys of the Rhondda Fawr and Rhondda Fach was just 542, but a century of coal-mining drew Welsh families in by the thousand and the population eventually reached over 160,000. The number of people in the valleys has fallen since the peak of the 1920s but the lines of houses ad shops still wind like ribbons along the hillsides in testimony to the great days of coal and the growing importance of light industry.

Overleaf: Cambridge has a history dating back to Roman times, but the present town dates to the time when two villages joined for mutual defence against the Vikings. Likewise, the university has its origins in a group of students who arrived here in 1209, but was not incorporated until many years later. The architecture of the colleges is as famous as their scholastic achievements, ranging from the many-pinnacled, mediaeval splendour of King's College Chapel to the starkly modern face of University Centre.

Lincoln Cathedral (previous pages) stands in a dominating position on its hill, high above the city's roofs and the surrounding fenland. The original Norman cathedral was damaged by an earthquake and much of the present church dates from the rebuilding undertaken in the 13th century. The great central tower, apart from standing to a height of 271 feet, is famous for its bell 'Great Tom of Lincoln' which weighs a staggering 5 tons.

The Lake District of northwestern England is one of the most scenically attractive regions in the country. Its craggy mountains, seen (these pages) around Rydal Water, are the remnants of a vast dome of rock thrown up some fifteen million years ago. The dome, centred around present-day Scafell, has since been eroded, particularly by glaciers over the past two million years, to form the present landscape of mountains and deep, sweeping valleys.

Rising high above the Firth of Clyde, Culzean Castle (overleaf) is the eighteenth-century home of the Earls of Cassillis. It was built around an earlier tower by Robert Adams in imitation of the Scottish Baronial style. His well-meant attempts at turrets, crenellations and machicolations were only spoilt by the strict adherence to symmetry which his Palladian background demanded.

Previous pages: the picturesque small town of Dumfries is rich in historical relics: the house where Robert Burns died still stands, as does the mausoleum in which he is interred. The many-arched, 15th-century bridge is still used by pedestrians, and a plaque in Bridge Street marks the spot where the Red Comyn was stabbed by Robert the Bruce in 1306.

More than any other man, Sir Walter Scott brought the idealised life of the Scottish Highlands into the public eye. He eulogised the lairds and clans who had followed Bonnie Prince Charlie to Culloden and romanticised their culture to such a degree that it became strangely attractive. He was no doubt responsible for the movement which caused Highland dress to become popular, brought the Royal Family to Balmoral and caused the revival of many Highland games and traditions. It is, therefore, appropriate that the home of this great man, Abbotsford (these pages), should have all the trappings of a Scottish Baronial Hall, whence the laird could manage his estates.

Overleaf: the great city of Edinburgh, capital of Scotland. The 16th-century palace of Holyroodhouse (foreground) stands beside the ruins of the thirteenth century Holyrood Abbey, within the walls of both have trod many distinguished and historic figures. Curving away from the Palace towards the formidable bulk of Edinburgh Castle is the Royal Mile, lined by fine and ancient buildings.

The great estuary of the Forth was for many years a barrier to communications in lowland Scotland, separating as it does two of the more populous regions of the country. In the 1880s the great engineering feat of bridging the firth was undertaken and the mighty cantilever rail bridge (previous pages) completed. The main spans are 1,710 feet across and stand 150 feet above the water. The suspension road bridge of 1964 finally replaced the ferry which had traversed the waters for 800 years.

These pages: the barren moors between Auchterarder and Strath Earn have a name which has earned them fame throughout the golfing world, Gleneagles. The golf courses which lie beside the Gleneagles Hotel are for many the mecca of the Royal and Ancient Game and are among the most famous in the world.

Overleaf: the fair city of Perth, which was created a Royal Burgh as early as 1210 and maintained its importance as a river port and capital of Scotland throughout the Middle Ages. In more recent centuries the town has depended more on its rich, agricultural hinterland and diversified, light industries. After a brief foray into history in 1715, when the Old Pretender was proclaimed king here, Perth slipped back into the gentle obscurity it has enjoyed ever since.

Isolated from any other town of importance by miles of mountains, glens and tortuous, winding roads, Inverness (previous pages) stands proudly on the River Ness. The strategic importance of the site has long been recognised, as witness the military installations, including a Royal castle of 1141, a Cromwellian fortress of 1652 and two great military roads built after the Jacobite rebellion of 1745. Today, its position has earned Inverness the sobriquet of 'capital of the Highlands' and an increasingly important role as a tourist centre.

In 1852 Prince Albert, consort of Queen Victoria, bought the Balmoral Estate for £31,000 as a Highland home for his wife, and had the house rebuilt to his own design in the Scottish Baronial style. The resultant mansion (these pages) has remained an occasional Royal residence ever since, with the Royal Family attending the nearby Braemar Games each summer.

Overleaf: winter's icy grip holds Loch Morlich in its chilly grasp. Beyond the lake the snow-clad heights of the Cairngorms roll away beneath a threatening sky heavy with snow.

Hadrian's wall (following page) runs from the Tyne to the Solway Firth, and marked the northern limit of the Roman Empire in Britain.